COPING WITH

Parents Who

Are Activists

Margot Webb

THE ROSEN PUBLISHING GROUP, INC./NEW YORK

Published in 1992 by The Rosen Publishing Group, Inc.
29 East 21st Street, New York, NY 10010

First Edition

Library of Congress Cataloging-in-Publication Data

Webb, Margot.
  Coping with parents who are activists / Margot Webb. —1st ed.
     p.   cm.
  Includes bibliographical references and index.
  Summary: Suggests ways to cope with parents who want to reshape society and the world, describes different kinds of activism, and discusses why parents choose to become involved.
  ISBN 0-8239-1416-X
  1. Social reformers—United States—Family relationships—Juvenile literature.   2. Political activists—United States—Family relationships—Juvenile literature.   3. Parent and child—United States—Juvenile literature.   [1. Reformers.   2. Political activists. 3. Parent and child.]   I. Title.
HN65.W395   1992
306.874—dc20   92-22136
                                                              CIP
                                                               AC

Manufactured in the United States of America

ABOUT THE AUTHOR ◊

argot Webb has been a teacher and a counselor to children in California, in the Los
Angeles area.

Born in Germany during the Holocaust, Mrs. Webb
managed to escape with her parents in 1939, but the rest
of her family died in Auschwitz.

Settling in California, Margot studied opera and was
fortunate enough to appear in a few productions. She
entered the University of Southern California with the
express purpose of continuing her musical career but was
waylaid by marriage. She and her husband, a Hindu from
India, lived for three years in Bombay before returning
to the United States.

Widowed, she first began to teach. She then took a
master's degree in counseling and began work on a
doctorate at the University of Southern California.
Remarried now, Mrs. Webb lives with her husband, an
editor, in the Los Padres Mountain region, fairly close
to Los Angeles.

Contents

Introduction

Tonight was the night! Jeff had prepared for weeks to tell his parents of his hope to go to a large Eastern university. They had wanted him to attend a Midwestern college. In fact, they had chosen it for him.

He knew all their objections. Other schools were too far away! Too expensive! Couldn't he try a smaller school first? It might be easier to make friends with the kind of people he'd grown up with. In his imagination, Jeff could hear his parents drone on and on.

Because of this, Jeff had decided to confront them only if he was accepted by the university of his choice.

Jeff worked hard on his project. His senior year in high school became a year of intense study.

Yesterday it had paid off! The principal had told Jeff that the university's dean of admissions had called to ask about him. The principal had given a glowing report. He had also mentioned that Jeff could use a scholarship.

"His parents can be proud of him," the dean had said. "We need bright, ambitious students to uphold our reputation. We have just the right scholarship for him."

Jeff kept the good news to himself for a full day. He practiced various ways to approach his mother and father and decided to discuss the situation after dinner the following evening.

When his father came home, Jeff noticed at once how

tired he looked. "He works too hard," Jeff thought. "Not having to pay for my tuition ought to be a relief for him."

His mother banged pots and pans around in the kitchen, muttering something about never getting any help, her high heels clicking over the tile floor.

"No!" Jeff thought. "If she's wearing high heels and she's complaining, that means she's in a rush to leave."

Quickly he went into the kitchen.

"How can I help you, Mom?" he asked.

"Dinner is ready—that's a fine time to ask," she blazed at him. "At least carry the food into the dining room."

"Michael," she called to her husband, who had trudged wearily upstairs to change into comfortable clothes. "You and Jeff will have to do the dishes tonight. I have a meeting for Lakeville Beautiful. I'm one of the main speakers."

Jeff put a dish of peas on the dining room table and spilled a few. His hands shook. He wondered if he could ever get a chance to talk to his parents when they were together.

"Mom, didn't you go to a meeting just last night?" He could hear the whine in his voice.

"That was a general meeting; this one is to acquaint several neighborhoods about ways to make our town a real showplace. No litter—plants, flowers, and trees everywhere. We even have twelve nurseries contributing to the cause." As she warmed to her subject, her voice took on a positive tone and her eyes glowed with pleasure at the evening to come.

"Hurry, Michael," she called once more.

"Couldn't you stay home tonight, please?" Jeff asked. "We need to have a family talk. I have something to tell you that might please you, something that will affect my entire future."

"What about your future?" his father asked as he came slowly down the stairs. "It sounds important. What do you say, Alice? Can you give up your meeting just tonight?"

"I guess my ideas and my life just aren't important enough around here. Why don't you two have your man-to-man talk, serve your own meal, and clean up after yourselves for a change. I've lost my appetite."

Jeff's mother took off her apron, fluffed her hair, shrugged quickly into her coat and ran out the door. He heard the car start up. It signaled the end of his news and views about life after high school.

"Sit down, Dad," Jeff said gently. "I'll serve dinner."

"Thanks, son. I'm really beat tonight. A contract that we worked hard on fell through this afternoon." He tried to smile. "Well, there's always a next time."

They ate in silence. Afterward Jeff did the dishes and told his dad to rest with the newspaper.

When he returned to the living room, his father was asleep in the overstuffed chair, and the middle section of the paper had fallen on the floor. As Jeff bent down to pick it up, he saw his mother's picture with a group of men and women all holding a garden tool in one hand and a small potted plant in the other.

"The Committee for 'Lakeville Beautiful' is a serious endeavor on the part of our citizens to make our town a more pleasant place to live," the article said. "Everyone is encouraged to pick up litter and to work in their yards and around the public square. Mrs. Smith, Mr. Albright, and others are all contributing their time . . ."

Jeff stopped reading.

He needed his parents' approval, he had assumed for months. Now he wasn't so sure. He'd be eighteen years old in August, one month before the semester at the university would begin. He could make his own decision.

But he'd never felt as alone as he did tonight.

Jeff's mother is an activist, someone who practices direct action in a cause that he or she believes in. Since you are reading this book, you've probably thought about the question of activism.

It is a large territory to contemplate—from "Lakeville Beautiful" to feeding the world's hungry. Activists want to reshape our society and our world. What they do may affect you and your future. What about the activists themselves? Certainly they're not all like Jeff's mother.

In this book you will learn about ways to cope with activist parents. You will also be confronted with many kinds of activism and with reasons parents choose to become involved.

You will face some difficult issues:

- Is the cause more important than my family?
- Am I still someone who counts at home?
- Am I being selfish by not supporting my parent in his or her search to help others?
- Does my parent use activism to escape family responsibility and boredom?
- Should I join my parent's activist group?
- How can the whole family find a solution to the separateness that often results from activism?

You are a growing member of our society, a person in your own right, a person with important needs, goals, and dreams for the future. It's only natural that at your age the main focus is on the help you still need from those around you—simple things like food, clothing, and shelter and also the more complex things like love, education, and opportunities. It is your right to expect these things from your family, your society, and your community.

And yet it's not too early for you to begin learning how to give back something to the world that supports you. This book is about finding the right balance between yourself and your family—yourself and your parents— yourself and the world. Coping with activist parents is an important first step in finding your own way in life.

P A R T ◇ I

WHAT IS AN ACTIVIST PARENT?

CHAPTER 1

Working for Change

If someone were to ask you how many groups you belong to, you might surprise yourself at the number. You belong first of all to your family group, to your class, and possibly groups within your class. Maybe you write for the school newspaper, or belong to a sports team, or help run student government.

Belonging to a group is part of the decision-making way of life. North Americans accomplish many things by getting people together.

There are businessmen's clubs whose purpose is to find ways of increasing profit. We find medical groups that function more effectively because they gather by specialty and have someone on hand at times of emergency.

There are bridge clubs, chess clubs, music groups, and many more.

The distinguishing feature of an activist group is that the activist wants to make a change in society. He or she, too, joins a group—most often political in nature—but the group works together to make a difference. The members see a threat to the well-being of others, such as in environmental issues, educational issues, racial issues, and many more.

Many activist parents work at community, state, and even federal levels to get their ideas across so that laws can be passed to help their cause.

The activist parent is not a "stay-at-home" type of person. He is busy with the group of choice in holding meetings and marches, writing newsletters, doing whatever is required to bring about change.

- Are your parents who are actively involved simply doing it for the good of others?
- Are you wondering if they get something out of being in their specific group?

Of course, they are! Their coworkers in the cause give them a sense of self-esteem, of doing something important instead of simply sitting back and grumbling about how things could be better. Your parents support a cause they deem fair and feel good about themselves. They belong to a group with which they can identify. They meet people who think as they do and thereby enlarge their circle of acquaintances.

Remember, the activist parent is not simply giving community service. He or she is dealing with making a definite change, the political part of which distinguishes it from other groups.

Nevertheless, your parent is not so different from many people in this country who are members of nonactivist organizations.

David's Interrupted Baseball Game

It was the summer of 1965, and David and his Babe Ruth League team were winning in the seventh inning.

Suddenly the park director came running across the field and spoke urgently to the coach.

Visiting parents as well as the teams were called together.

"There's been a riot in Watts," the coach said. (Watts is a section in the heart of Los Angeles, California.) "Even though we're twenty miles away in the San Fernando Valley, we suggest that you all go home."

No amount of groaning from the teams stopped parents from taking the boys away from the park.

David and his friend, Peter, climbed in the car. They lived across the street from each other and had been close ever since 6th grade.

"What's this riot about?" David asked his mother, who was driving. She explained that the people in Watts were poor and didn't have the same opportunities that white people did. She hastened to add that Dr. Martin Luther King would not approve of rioting to solve problems.

For the first time David, who was black, and Peter, who wasn't, looked at each other with a touch of insecurity.

"Do you still like me?" Peter asked.

"Why not—you're not responsible," David answered somewhat shakily.

During the next few days the boys became inseparable, sleeping at each other's houses, watching fires raging in Watts on TV. They saw the destruction of stores and the looting.

The boys' fathers got together and talked for a long time. They decided that once everything calmed down they would have to do something to help—and they did. They joined an activist group called Fair Housing. It worked to find appropriate apartments or houses for people regardless of race and to enforce existing laws against discrimination.

David's and Peter's mothers also decided to join, and three times a week they worked with Fair Housing.

Finally, they along with citizens of Watts formed a program in which youngsters from Watts came to the San Fernando Valley to spend a weekend with a friendly family, and the following week children from San Fernando visited in Watts.

Both sets of parents remained active for years to come in the fight for equality, joining several organizations.

The boys were proud of their parents and didn't mind the time taken from them. They could play in the Babe Ruth League with greater confidence, knowing that their folks worked toward an ideal. There were enough people in the bleachers to cheer them on, even if their parents were not there.

Moreover, they'd made friends in Watts during their weekends there and looked forward to their visits. Both boys were enriched by their experiences through their parents' activism.

Now grown men, David and Peter are still close. They remember with respect the way their parents responded in a time of crisis.

The activist parent cannot be described in one dimension. Emotional and psychological factors enter into reasons for becoming involved in change. These will be discussed throughout the book.

You, as the son or daughter of an activist, lead a more complex life than the child of a parent who prefers to relax at home, even though that parent, too, may wish for changes in our society.

You have more to deal with and quite a bit to think about. You are a part of a group called family, and your feelings, as much as your input, count.

CHAPTER 2

Like Father, Like Son?

You may tell yourself, "It's fine with me if my father is an activist, but I still want him at home often enough to be a father."

Sounds reasonable enough. However, you may have a problem if your father's idea of being with you is to have you join in his activism and become a contributing member.

"We can be together much more if you come to meetings with me," he may tell you.

If his group doesn't interest you, how can you handle the situation without becoming estranged from him?

First of all, you are undoubtedly aware as a teenager that you are shifting somewhat from your parents' value system to your own. If you have a strong sense of self-confidence, you may not need constant parental approval. You can talk with your father (or mother) about the fact that you understand his activism in whatever cause he's taken on, but your interests lie elsewhere. Such a conflict can be handled far more easily if you take an attitude of learning. Let him explain what he means, rather than blaming him or resisting. You don't want a power struggle in which you give up and join your father's group in the hope of keeping his love. You may be afraid to tell your parent how you feel, but think about all the hours you'll spend doing something you don't want to do if you keep quiet.

Marilyn Ferguson wrote in *The Aquarian Conspiracy*: "Fear is a question. What are you afraid of, and why? Our fears are a treasure house of self-knowledge if we explore them."

Going against your father's wish may cause you some anxiety or sadness. You've had some of these sensations before as a result of emotional pain: a stinging in the eyes, a quiver of the chin, a lump in the throat. The pain comes from the fear of being rejected by your father, who really wants to share his activism with you while spending time with you. He likes to tell friends, "Like father, like son . . . we work together as a team." If you are not excited by his cause, tell him so. How can you cope with his disappointment?

Talk to your father about his beliefs. Try to understand him by discussing him with other members of the family. Once you've reached an understanding of why your father wants you to be with him, you may realize that he did what he thought was best without harming you.

You can ask him to spend time with you by doing other things you both enjoy. Of course, that time might be shorter than you'd like it to be.

Quality time is more important than quantity. Your father needs to hear about your values, too. Your relationship with him will blossom as each of you brings the richness of your separate experiences to your discussions.

You may wonder at this point how the phrases "like father, like son" or "like mother, like daughter" came to be. Was it an assumption on the part of the parents, a type of selfishness? Not at all. Let's take a look at the history of parent-son and -daughter relationships.

Long ago, children went to school for only a few years, and formal education played a minor role in the average family. Working along with a parent was far more important than schooling.

Parents taught their children as they worked beside them. This formed a strong bond, and the expectation was that children would follow in their parents' footsteps. Children looked up to their fathers and mothers because they were so important to them. Parents, in turn, found their work made easier not only because the children helped, but because they were so greatly appreciated. The child felt secure and loved because of the parents' extending themselves to teach him. At the same time, the parent who was admired, actually "honored," could not do otherwise than love his child.

So most sons and daughters followed in the footsteps of their elders. When a son inherited the farm or business, the father knew his son carried on where he had left off. It was like a promise of the continuance of life. The father's work would not end with his death.

Today, everything changes so fast that it is unrealistic to expect a son to follow in the occupation of his father. Possibly that occupation will no longer exist in a few years, high tech having taken its place. Sons and daughters seldom have the experience of seeing their parents at work. In fact, they have trouble at times in describing it.

So it is understandable that parent and child need to do something else together to form a close human relationship.

You as a teenager still need the emotional tie to family. Perhaps one way to get it is to follow your parents' footsteps in one of their causes and become involved, if and *only* if your interests are like theirs. They may have taught you early on, or you may have observed the value of their activism. Encouraged by them, having seen their joy in the work, you may indeed not be offended by the phrases "like father, like son," or "like mother, like daughter."

CHAPTER 3

Hidden Costs of

Activism

P eople become activists for many reasons. Some may not be easily noticed at first because of a "hidden agenda."

Having a hidden agenda is giving a public reason for doing something (such as being an activist) when inwardly the reason is solving a painful personal problem.

Tom's Hidden Agenda

Tom's father was a successful surgeon, and his mother was becoming a fairly well-known artist.

Tom's sister was attending Yale University after winning numerous academic honors.

It seemed to Tom that to be an admired member of the family one had to be a winner. No one had ever told him that, it was his feeling. However, he was an average student and had never done anything he considered "spectacular."

"It isn't enough just to be their son," he often mused unhappily. He had to find something to make his family notice him. He knew he'd never be an A student.

His favorite activity was running. He was fast, and he didn't have to think his unhappy thoughts while his body was engaged in strenuous activity. He also enjoyed running alone in the nearby woods and filling his lungs with the good smells of pine trees.

One day his P.E. teacher noticed Tom's ability and asked him to join the track team. Tom really had little interest in the team, but he realized that if he excelled, won trophies, became a sort of hero in school, his parents might let him into their select "winners group." Tom agreed to join the team.

He told everyone enthusiastically that he had always enjoyed running and was happy about being selected for track. His hidden agenda, however, was to win approval from his parents.

Let's take a look at how your family's hidden agenda might affect you and your siblings when your mother and father become activists.

Let's suppose your parents have been activists for the last four years. Before that, it seems to you, a great deal more closeness existed. You and your younger sister talked at dinner about school, friends, and even problems. Your parents were willing to listen, even if they didn't always have a solution. Just having them around proved comforting. They were mother and father. You, as their children, were treated as the most important people in their lives.

When you were thirteen and your sister was twelve, your parents became activists in an important political cause. They explained their reasons for joining the group.

"We are moral, ethical people, and we have to do our best to make our world a better place," your father said.

"We are working for a better future for you children," your mother added. "Also, you're old enough to stay by yourselves once in a while."

At first, both you and your sister were pleased and proud. Your parents were out there doing something. They didn't just sit in front of the TV like so many other parents.

However, when their activism ballooned to three evenings each week, you began to feel pushed aside. You and your sister still liked the idea of having your parents around, even if you didn't want to spend all your free time with them.

Also, you noticed the excitement that was generated between your mother and father whenever it was time for a meeting. You and your sister wondered, "Could there be a hidden agenda?"

"I've noticed that Mom and Dad are getting along so well," your sister confided. "They're so close."

"Yeah," you replied, "ever since they became involved in their meetings, they seem to have a lot to talk about."

Maybe they needed a place to go where they were both appreciated, where their work benefited society, and where they felt good about themselves and each other. Their hidden agenda was to perk up their marriage.

You and your sister asked your mother how it was when she was growing up. Did she have her parents around, and could she talk about her dreams and problems?

"In my day a child's feelings seemed to count for very little," she said. "My family would say, 'But she's only a kid; what does she know? The way she carries on, you'd think the world was coming to an end.' When I was a child I got the definite impression that my ideas and feelings were not to be taken seriously until I was grown-up. I was used to hearing: 'It's silly to feel that way', or 'You have no reason to be so upset', or even 'You're making a big fuss over nothing'."

If your parents were brought up that way, they may not realize that you don't feel right about their activism, which makes you feel left out.

Insist on finding out why your parents need three nights a week for meetings. Is their frequent presence of such importance to the cause? Ask them how the meetings help *them*. Try to bring the hidden agenda out into the open. Tell them that you miss them.

They may answer, "Now you're teenagers. You can't go through life depending on us for everything. You're wonderful kids, with lots of friends. Why don't you call them, have them come over and spend a few evenings?"

You may be angry because your friends *have* been coming over. Your friends are not mother and father, you can point out.

In your discussion with your folks, tell them that activism is fine, that you admire the cause and their doing something about their convictions. But point out that you are upset because activism has become *the thing* and family closeness suffers. Don't be afraid to tell them that you're hurt.

Perhaps a compromise can be reached. Some of the work for the cause could be done at home, or one week-end day could be set aside for family outings.

Being aware of the hidden agenda will allow you to cope by understanding that you and your sister are not purposely pushed aside. The hidden agenda has nothing to do with you or your sister. Your parents are working on a problem, and your openness with them may allow them to face the real issues and bring the family close again.

Fear of Being Alone

You may wonder what the fear of being alone may have to do with your parents' becoming activists.

It is not the fear of being abandoned. It has to do with something that every human being experiences—and the way each of us handles it accounts for our many differences.

As people grow up, they begin to realize that they are individuals. There is no one in the world exactly like them. In a way, that's a scary thought, and it causes some anxiety and fear.

Can you remember the first time you felt you were different from your mom or dad? You realized that you were a separate human being apart from them. No longer were you the little boy or girl whose whole life centered around them, whose Mommy and Daddy could fix everything.

Janie in the Pool

It was a hot summer day when Janie, age five, and her parents were invited for a swim and barbecue at a neighbor's home.

Janie loved the water. She liked its coolness as she floated on her back while watching clouds slowly drift by.

When her family arrived at the neighbor's house, a big party was in progress. About ten children, some her age, were already splashing in the pool, playing "Marco Polo," throwing beach balls, and screaming with pleasure.

"Go on in," Janie's mother said, "but stay at the shallow end."

Janie hesitantly made her way to the pool. A teenager acting as lifeguard encouraged her down the steps into the water. As she began to float on her back, two girls came up and splashed her.

"Stop it," she cried, "I just want to float for a while."

"How boring," the girls laughed and went away.

All of a sudden Janie felt very much alone. She wasn't like the others.

But she decided to continue floating. She was a little afraid but at the same time sensed that she had the power to do what she wanted to do.

After a while, however, Janie was again overcome with the feeling of being different and wanted to become part of the splashing group of kids. She stopped floating and played happily with the others. She needed to be part of her world.

You, too, probably have conflicts about being alone or joining the world outside. You can do either one whenever the mood strikes you, but you don't want to lose your sense of self, of being the person you and only you are.

Your activist parent has the same problem. It is part of being human. He may have found a worthy cause, one that will benefit his world and possibly yours. He throws his heart and soul into it. The fear of his aloneness as an individual is temporarily hidden. He feels safe while engaged in his activism.

You are aware of times when the knowledge that you are the only *you* in the world is almost too much to bear. Joining others in a game or in some other activity relieves the awesomeness of this.

Your parents also have such moments. Instead of

splashing in a pool or playing a game, they perform and fulfill a special role in society.

How can you cope with your parents' unspoken motives for becoming activists? Compare your individual alone self with your need to be part of a group.

Your parents have this need, as you do. It may merely be expressed differently.

Coping with your activist parents may mean letting them go a little and taking the journey of "becoming" partly by yourself.

PART ⋄ II

HOW DO YOU FEEL?

CHAPTER 4

Positive Feelings

Many teenagers, possibly you among them, are proud of their parents' involvement in a cause. They realize that many people become activists not because they have a hidden agenda, but because they have hopes for the future as well as for the present.

Adam Werbach

Adam is an eighteen-year-old who grew up in a family of activists. His father and mother, both professional people, constantly strove for new approaches in their respective fields of medicine and education, according to Adam.

Adam cannot recall feeling anger or feeling left out by his parents' busy lives. Instead, he is grateful for the outstanding role models his father and mother created for him. He says he was brought up in an ethical home where he learned early about the need to help in making the world a better place.

It became natural for Adam to become an activist. He found a cause of his own as a student environmental activist with the Sierra Club.

He started a recycling program at his school in California with the help of other students and faculty sponsors. It was so good that Harvard-Westlake School became a model for high school recycling programs nationwide. Adam also leads environmental workshops like Camp Alonim, a summer camp where he started and continues to manage an environmental program.

With a grant from the Sierra Club, Adam is planning a leadership training program. This will give seventy-five student activists from around the country a week-long retreat to learn the skills to help them achieve their goals.

Adam received the Vote Environment 1990 Best Volunteer Award and is considered one of the Sierra Club's most valuable resources.

"Sierra Club and I, we're a perfect match," he says.

In Adam's case, the positive feelings he has toward his parents' activism are clearly returned by his father and mother. This family of activists chose their own causes, which brought them closer together.

If a family works together and takes pride in each other's achievements, activism can be a big plus. You meet new people, learn new things, and can give to life.

Coping with activist parents (as well as their coping with your cause) can be a positive and warm way to interact. If you listen with empathy, you may feel their enthusiasm. They may appreciate your patience with their busy lives and, in turn, be glad to hear what you have to say about your cause.

You, too, can find "the perfect match" as Adam did— not only in your activism, but with your family, as well.

Coping with One Another

Positive, warm feelings often come about when your parents encourage your sense of morality and values.

Your mother and father, as good role models, are aware of your perceptions of the world.

Thomas Lickona, a professor of education at the State University of New York at Cortland, says, "I think the capacity for goodness is there [in a child] from the start."

That's a great thing to hear, but still you want your parents to help you nurture those "good" instincts, just as they help you in becoming a good reader, athlete, or musician.

Coping with parents is made much easier if they *explain* their reasons for being activists rather than expecting you to go along simply because they are adults and "said so!"

In homes where ideas, rules, and feelings are *explained* and *justified*, as opposed to being laid down without explanation, you as the son or daughter are more likely to have positive thoughts about your parents.

Explanations give a sense of security. Ask for them, if they are not freely given. Your show of interest may open the door to better understanding, particularly if you are not in agreement with the special activism for which your folks work.

Studies have shown that if you grow up in a home where explanations are given and open discussions are a part of family life, you are more likely to become a leader in school: self-directed and eager to learn. Also, it is easier to absorb your parents' values.

Sara

From the time Sara was a little girl, she loved animals. With her mother's help she became an activist at age four.

During a trip to the zoo in New York, Sara learned about endangered species and wanted to help.

Sara and her mother baked cakes and cookies and sold them in front of her apartment house. She was excited when she had collected $35, which she sent right away to the World Wildlife Fund.

Imagine her disappointment when a few weeks later a letter arrived asking for more money. The little girl thought she had solved the problem of all the animals in the world.

Her mother, however, patiently explained to her daughter that many big problems require the help of lots of people.

The explanation worked!

Sara, now nine years old, has expanded her activism. Through her school, she helps out at an inner-city child-care center. She also regularly takes meals to homeless people in her neighborhood.

Because of her sensitive mother, Sara can adjust to the idea that a one-time contribution may be just the beginning of solving a problem.

Her mother helped her on the road of causes in which *Sara* was interested. Actually, she became Sara's "partner."

A positive attitude such as the one Sara and her mother had toward each other came about through explanation as well as talking things out. Activism lent itself to a wonderful relationship between Sara and her mother.

Negative Feelings

S adly, not all families function in ways that make members feel good about themselves. In this part, we shall explore different types of behavior—yours as well as your parents'—to discover what could be causing tensions in your relationships. Let's start with you: Are you jealous of your parents' activism? They have something to do that leaves you out. Nothing you do seems as worthwhile as their activism, and you have a sense of abandonment because they are not at home as often as they used to be. Suppose you go to your best friend to complain. He doesn't like to see you unhappy, and he tries to divert your attention from the problem with assurances, jokes, comfort, and so on.

Your friend is trying his best but is unknowingly preventing you from fully experiencing your anger and aloneness. You need to experience it before you can accept it and grow into a more complete, integrated human being.

Your friend is using the equivalent of a Band-aid on a big wound.

You are not a weak person, and you want help and

understanding, but it has to come in a different form. So much of your time is spent in manipulating yourself and your mother and father that you have very little energy to cope with the world. You need your energy for self-support, rather than support from others. Amazingly, you will discover that you can do exciting things for yourself, things you thought you needed your parents to do for you. You have a great deal of unused potential. Most people are much more capable, more intelligent, stronger, and more able than they imagine.

"But I still need my parents," you may answer. You are right. The question is whether you need them as much as you did when you were younger?

Whatever your experience is, you have to begin where you are and start your journey of self-discovery from that point.

The "Why" Question

Have you asked your parents, "Why do you have to be activists? Why can't we all go bowling the way we used to?"

Are you honestly asking those questions to gain information? Or is it possible that you are not asking a question at all, but making a disguised statement such as, "I don't like your being involved in your cause all the time. I wish you'd quit."

Don't trap yourself in "why" questions to cope with your experience of jealousy or embarrassment.

Allow yourself and your parents to clear the air by each saying exactly what you mean. Other questions that lead to arguments rather than to solutions begin with:

"What if . . . ?"
"How come . . . ?" (a disguised *why* question)
"Do we have to?"

Another snare is, "I'd like to ask mother . . ." (or father). That is sure to anger the parent who is being left out.

You need to become reacquainted with your parents and yourself. One way to start a lively conversation in which no one blames anyone is to have the family participate in a little exercise. Make up sheets of paper for everyone entitled, "The Real Me Response Sheet." Give everyone a pen and tell them to circle the word that describes them best in each sentence.

The Exercise

1. I am more indoor than outdoor.
2. I am more fast than slow.
3. I am more past than present.
4. I am more yes than no.
5. I am more on the ground than in the air.
6. I am more a thinker than a doer.
7. I am more a hamburger than a steak.
8. I am more a leader than a follower.
9. I am more a single tree than a forest.
10. I am more a sports car than a Model T.
11. I am more a log cabin than a condominium.
12. I am more a frown than a smile.
13. I am more a morning person than a night person.
14. I am more an ear than a mouth.

After everyone has finished, give each person one or two of the following questions. Have the prepared questions, folded, in a bowl from which you all pick. Everyone participates in answering the questions.

1. How did you feel when I asked you to do this activity?
2. How are you feeling about sharing your answers?
3. Did any of your answers make you want to talk more about it, to explain?
4. Did you find any difference in your reasons for being in the same category as Mom or me. (If you included brothers or sisters, add them.)
5. Did you feel uncomfortable making a decision?
6. What similarities did you find that were common to us as a family?

If your family is willing to do this exercise with you, chances are you'll all learn something about each other you hadn't thought of. It is a positive exercise, and the way you listen to your parents' responses, as well as they do to yours, may open the door to let out some of those negative, angry feelings.

Guilty Feelings

Feelings of guilt take up much valuable time and are extremely destructive. Let's take a look at what could be happening inside you.

You are angry and hurt, jealous of the time your parents' activism takes. At the same time you may have a sense of guilt. An inner voice may tell you that you are selfish in your anger because of your needs. You still seek the approval, not just the companionship, of your parents.

First of all, you must learn to forgive yourself. You are at an age when you are almost an adult but still need advice from your parents. There's nothing wrong with that. Your anxiety can be caused by many factors.

Bill's Dad

It was a warm, sunny spring day. Bill and his parents had just finished breakfast, and everyone bustled about the house.

"Where's my briefcase?" Bill's father shouted in frustration. His mother laughed, winked at Bill, and told him she had put it near the front door, because the hunt for the briefcase had become a daily occurrence.

Bill ran upstairs to get his books and when he came down saw his parents kissing each other good-bye.

"You're a terrible tease," his father smiled fondly at his mother.

"And you have your head in the clouds," she responded, patting his cheek.

Both parents noticed Bill on the stairs at the same time.

"You'll be late for school," his father admonished.

"How can I interrupt you two lovebirds?" Bill laughed.

The morning was off to a good start.

Bill's dad left the house, started the car, and drove off to his job at an insurance company.

Bill waved once more to his mother, who stood in the doorway watching him meet two friends.

She planned to spend the morning in a shelter for abused women, doing record-keeping.

Bill's world came to a halt only an hour later. In his first-period science class he was called to the office. The principal told him softly, "I will drive you to Memorial Hospital. Your dad's been in an accident. Your mother has already been contacted and is on her way there."

"Is it serious?" Bill's whole body shook.

"Let's hope not . . ." the principal answered vaguely.

At the hospital, Bill ran up the stairs to the information

booth. His mother was waiting for him, a bewildered look in her eyes.

"Dad is gone," she whispered, holding her arms out to her son. The unbelievable had happened.

It seemed to Bill that life in his house began to take on many changes after the funeral.

At first his mother and he were close and cried together—clung to each other, comforted each other.

Somewhere deep inside, Bill began to be aware of an enormous anger toward his father. How could he have left the family? Bill felt more and more sorry for himself.

Finally his mother had to go to work. She had been an accountant before her marriage, and she returned to her previous occupation with a good income. Bill was alone much of the time. His chores around the house increased. His mother often went to bed early, exhausted.

A year later, she announced that she intended to give two evenings a week to her cause for abused women. She told Bill she had joined a group that worked for legislation to protect women from the men who abused them and their children.

"I thought you were so tired," he responded angrily.

"I was, Bill, but part of my tiredness is mourning for Dad. I need to do something besides work. I want to help these women. They deserve better lives."

Part of Bill understood what his mother meant, but his angry self was jealous. "I'm not enough for her," he told himself, although he himself was seldom at home with various school activities.

Would she take the car all the time now? he wondered. How would he be able to get out for football practice or a date? Why didn't these abused women just get a divorce? he asked himself. Didn't he and his mother have enough trouble without worrying about an issue he didn't really understand?

How often have you been resentful of your parents' lives away from you? If you think you're not being reasonable, guilt follows all too often.

Ask yourself what is the underlying cause of your angry and sad feelings.

In Bill's case, he had not come to terms with his father's death. His mother's absence from home because of her work and later her activism seemed to Bill to be yet another loss.

Does This Fit You?

Whenever you haven't been sure of yourself, you have needed approval and support. You probably received both from your parents when you were younger. They were there for you.

Now as a teenager, if they are very occupied with work and their cause, you may begin to think no one cares about you. You wonder angrily if you even exist for your mom and dad, since they don't seem to notice you.

You would almost welcome some disapproval just to get their attention. Perhaps your actions show your rage at them: not doing well at school, or slamming doors around the house. You become defensive, in the hope that they'll worry about you.

Whatever feelings you have are okay—anger, disappointment, or a temporary regression to temper tantrums. Your feelings are the barometer of your emotions. Ask yourself:

- What do I gain from my anger?
- Will it change my parents? Probably not.

Suppose you approached the problem with understanding of their situation. You wouldn't think of yourself
constantly, but of the people in your family. How might
that change the relationship you have with them? Can you
think of some benefit to you from your understanding?

Your world is expanding. As a teenager you can turn to
friends, teachers, coaches, and other sympathetic people
who may be able to clarify your predicament.

Only you can choose and weigh the benefits of your
strong emotions. Your actions and the reactions of your
parents and friends will show you how you are coping.

Do Your Parents Embarrass You?

There are times when your parents' activism can embarrass you. If your mother or father joins your school
PTA, it probably won't bother you. Your friends' parents
are PTA members, too. Meetings are usually held in the
evenings, or in the mornings in the auditorium away
from classrooms and student activities.

PTA members often concern themselves with helping
their particular school. However, some members become
activists seeking to change the system not only in one
school, but in a district or even a state. These activists
often have excellent ideas, but they must be careful not
to embarrass their own children.

Mrs. Robinson's "New Career"

Mrs. Robinson worked as a mathematician before she and
her husband adopted Jeremy and Judy. Jeremy was a
first-grader and Judy a sixth-grader.

As soon as the adoptions became final, Mrs. Robinson
quit her job and became a PTA member. Unfortunately,

Judy was a poor student. Mrs. Robinson was certain that it had to be the teacher's fault. She began to go to class and observe her new daughter.

Judy's face turned red every time her mother entered the classroom. She begged her not to do it anymore. She'd try harder, she said, and cried a good deal. Finally, Mrs. Robinson stopped her visits, but she was sure her little Judy was not to blame for her poor grades. The fault had to be the teacher's.

Mrs. Robinson started visiting other classrooms, including Jeremy's. Jeremy had no trouble learning, but on the days his mother came to class he refused to join the other children in their activities.

Mrs. Robinson worked hard for the PTA and within six months was elected president. This gave her an excuse to be at school daily. She ate with the teachers in the faculty room and listened to their conversations, hoping to hear something about her children.

As president, Mrs. Robinson decided that some teachers should be fired, the math books were too difficult, the music lessons were boring. The school, she felt, needed a complete overhaul.

She began visiting other schools and finally made her way to the Board of Education. She appeared on TV, telling everyone who cared to listen how awful the education was in many schools. Mrs. Robinson determined to visit the state capital and take her complaints to the Superintendent of Schools.

Jeremy and Judy were teased at school every day.

"Hey, Judy, where's your mom?" children shouted.

"Jeremy's a sissy. His mother wants to be with him every second," others screamed.

"Did you see the new TV star last night?" a boy asked Judy, "she looked just like your busybody mom."

Although friends tried to advise Mrs. Robinson that she was hurting her children with her activism, she thought she was doing the right thing. She continued her crusade through Judy's junior high school.

Judy couldn't wait to leave home and ran away in tenth grade. She was found a year later, living in a home for unwed mothers and expecting a baby. Refusing to return to school, she stayed with her mother (whose husband had divorced her) for a few months. Then Judy put the baby up for adoption and ran off again with her boyfriend.

Jeremy went to his father after Judy had left for the second time and begged to live with him. Mr. Robinson gladly agreed.

Mrs. Robinson continues to work for her cause of better education in the public schools.

- Can you think of a way Judy could have handled her embarrassment?
- Was she responsible for her mother's behavior?
- Do you think Jeremy's idea of living with his father was a good one?

Often parents like Mrs. Robinson engage in a power struggle not only with the children, but with the husband as well. Such people have a need to be in control. They don't listen to others. Mr. Robinson left and divorced his wife not because she was an activist, but because she chose an area in which the children suffered from her constant interference in their lives.

Jeremy and Judy had trouble trusting their mother. They both held back from being open with her because they couldn't trust her. Trust means feeling able to predict their parents' responses and being sure that they themselves won't be hurt. That kind of certainty is hard to find.

Jeremy clearly trusted *his own* feelings and was able to get away from his mother.

Judy, on the other hand, was so deeply hurt that she lost her self-esteem and self-respect. She felt rejected by her mother because she was constantly reminded of her poor grades. She couldn't live up to her mother's image, and she ran away because she was anxious and unhappy.

Was there a way for her to cope better with Mrs. Robinson's misplaced activism?

The only way was to face the pain of embarrassment squarely. Pain has its own limits and may have to be experienced several times before the deep pain is released. If Jeremy and Judy had been closer in years, they could have supported each other more. Support by someone we love actually heals our wounds. Once healing takes place, we are freer.

CHAPTER 6

The Pressure To
Conform

Frequently parents have very strong feelings on issues they consider moral and ethical.

Often such parents insist that their children follow their example. One of the problems that bring activists to heated discussion is the decision about abortion. Parents on both sides of the issue believe that their position is the correct one.

Recently a parade was held by a group of activists who want to abolish abortion. In the parade were children, some only five years old, wearing signs proclaiming, "I wouldn't be here if an abortionist had killed me." Did these children know what the signs said? Surely the five-year-olds had no idea. How about the older children? Did they know the meaning of abortion? Did they really want to be in such a parade? Those youngsters were used by their parents, whether the issue of abortion is right or wrong. How might they feel as they grow older and continue to be pressured to conform to their parents' stand on abortion?

Instead of pressure, it would have been better had the parents explained their "right to life" cause to their children. If the children had understood the cause, perhaps they would have joined it willingly.

Let's say your parents are pressuring you to conform to their beliefs on activism. Since the abortion issue is of national interest, let's use it as an example. Let's look at both sides before you make a decision.

Each year more than 6 million American women become pregnant, and more than 1.6 million have abortions. Do these women have the right to control their own bodies?

Roe Versus Wade

This famous case is one the most controversial decisions the United States Supreme Court ever handed down.

The case was decided in 1973. The High Court declared that a woman has a right to have an abortion during the first three months of pregnancy or at any time her health is in danger. The state in which the woman lives has no right to stop her or influence her. In 1989, however, the Supreme Court heard a case entitled Missouri versus Webster Reproductive Health Services. This case concerned a 1989 Missouri law that prohibited abortion in public facilities and forbade public employees to counsel women about abortion.

In April both supporters and opponents of abortion rights watched the court carefully. When the trial date came close, abortion rights activists were afraid, while anti-abortion activists hoped the case would mean the end of Roe vs. Wade.

In July the Court reached its decision. It ruled that the state of Missouri had the right to restrict abortions.

The Roe decision was weakened, because each state was free to decide for itself if abortion would be legal. So fifty states now could have fifty sets of standards.

Since then, thirty-six states have required teenagers to involve their parents if they decide to have an abortion.

The organizations against abortion are called "pro-life." The pro-life activists believe that a fetus (unborn baby) has life, and therefore abortion is murder. These activists include among their supporters President George Bush and former President Ronald Reagan.

The groups who are for abortion rights call themselves "pro-choice." They believe that a woman's body is her own and the government has no right to interfere in her decision. They are not specifically for abortion but believe that it is a woman's right to decide whether to continue a pregnancy or end it.

You may now wonder, when does life really begin? Does it begin the moment a man's sperm joins with a woman's egg?

Philosophers and scientists have argued about that for hundreds of years.

Scientists argue that when a heart starts beating and brain activity begins, life has probably started.

But scientists cannot say when a human soul enters a fetus.

So the argument goes on between pro-life and pro-choice activists.

Becky Bell

Becky Bell was a 17-year-old girl who discovered in 1988 that she was pregnant. After thinking about what she could do, she went to the Indianapolis office of Planned Parenthood to see if she could get an abortion. She was told that under Indiana law she would have to inform her parents.

Becky was very upset. She didn't want to hurt her mother and father by telling them that she was pregnant.

One night Becky told her parents that she was going to a party, but she really went to an illegal abortionist.

When Becky came home that night she began to hemorrhage, her lungs filled with fluid, and she died.

Becky's father blames the law for his daughter's death.

But in many places in America people think, "Thousands of unborn children are murdered each year by teenagers who aren't mature enough to know what they're doing." That is a direct quote from John Paul Wauk, of *Human Life Review*.

Each year over one million teenagers become pregnant. Nearly half choose to have abortions.

But in thirty-six states the law requires that they must get their parents' permission first.

Suppose your parents are pro-choice and want you to conform to their ideas and to help their activities. They are convinced that they could save the lives of teenagers if abortion were legal in all states.

Although you have a feeling for the pro-life argument, your parents pressure you to help. They insist that you at least address envelopes to send letters to politicians in an effort to change the laws.

Each time you address a letter, you feel terrible and helpless. What will happen?

1. Your parents make demands.

2. You pay no attention to your negative feelings and do what they ask.
3. Anger creeps in.
4. Anger comes out.
5. Someone gets hurt.
6. The family suffers.

You must protect *yourself*. Speak out. If your parents become furious, don't doubt yourself. Simply repeat how you feel. Tell them you'll help them in other ways. Your parents may not agree with you, but they probably will respect you for *your* ideas. Always try to use reason when stating your side of an issue. No one listens in a shouting match. Think through your ideas. You might even take notes, which will show your family how serious you are.

- Do you believe that pro-choice and pro-life activists have valid points?
- Why is the issue of abortion so difficult to decide?
- Why does the abortion issue engage so many activists and politicians?
- Do you think the pressure to conform is fair?

CHAPTER 7

Positive/Negative
Feelings

So far, we have discussed your positive feelings toward your parents' activism and your negative ones. It need not be an either-or situation. It is possible to have partially positive and partially negative feelings.

The big question is, how do you handle them? An interesting story of a family of activists is told in a movie (available in video) called "A World Apart."

The story takes place in South Africa in 1963. South Africa practices a policy called *apartheid*, or separation between black people and white people. At that time, blacks were used as servants or workers by the whites who had taken over their land, and they were not allowed to live dignified lives. The movie shows how the police terrorized and dehumanized the black citizens of South Africa.

A journalist, Diana Roth, became an activist for the

cause of black rights. She and her husband put themselves and their three children at great risk.

Mr. Roth left South Africa to spread the word about the evil happenings in his country. There was a question about whether he could return home safely or would be killed.

The oldest daughter was teased and humiliated at school about her father, and later about her mother. Her best friend was no longer allowed to play with her.

Finally her mother, who was working with black activists, was arrested. She was the first white woman to go to solitary confinement under the 90-Day Detention Act, which authorized holding a person prisoner for three months without a trial.

Alone in a cell, Diana is "A World Apart" from home, friends, and her lonely young daughter, who was struggling to grow up in a land of hatred and injustice.

How did the oldest girl handle the situation with her activist parents? Mostly, she was sad and afraid. However, she clung to a black woman for comfort. She went to her part of town and to a meeting of black activists. There she saw the police beating the activists and she came to understand why her mother and father had to try to help change the laws.

Here is a case in which a young girl has both positive and negative feelings. She knows that her "aloneness" is caused by her parents' leaving home to pursue their ideals. Yet she understands that change is necessary to avoid terror and injustice.

- If you were a parent in a country like South Africa, would it be more important to you to keep your family quiet and "safe" and go along with the mainstream? Or would you feel the need to become an activist and work toward equality between the races?

- If you have no definite answer, you probably have both positive and negative feelings about what to do: the safety of your family versus ultimately the safety of everyone. What could you do about these divergent feelings? How would you handle the issue?

Think of these struggles within yourself as a gift, because you are in the process of forming your realistic self.

Your self-image cannot be completed all at once. Think of your self-image as wet cement. Imagine that each of your struggles with positive and negative feelings leaves a mark and shapes your character. As long as you view your thoughts with honesty, you'll have no regrets as the cement hardens and becomes a permanent part of your emerging adult personality.

Bilingual Activism

For many years our schools did not help students who came from foreign countries. The theory of *immersion* was popular. Immersion means placing a student in a totally English-speaking environment.

Many Spanish-speaking, Korean-speaking, and other foreign-born Americans became activists and wanted their children to be taught in their native language during part of the day and to absorb English the rest of the time. The activists held that their children should not fall behind in math, science, and geography just because they did not understand English.

Many parents became activists on the other side of the issue. They asserted that in the United States people speak English, and newcomers should learn the language of the country immediately.

Many of you have attended bilingual classes. Perhaps your parents are activists for or against bilingualism.

Again, you may have had both positive and negative feelings about it.

As a newcomer to the United States you may not want to be singled out while the teacher speaks your language to only five or six students in your class. As you hear English more and more, however, you pick it up, and soon your language skills are tested. You now can do all your lessons in English, and yet you haven't fallen behind academically.

- How do you feel now about your parents' activism toward bilingual education?
- Which seemed more important to you—not being embarrassed when you first entered an American school, or being caught up in all your subjects by the time you had learned English?

On the other hand, some activists insist that immersion is the quickest way to learn any language. Teaching children math in Spanish, the activists say, ensures that they will spend their lives in the Rio Grande Valley. Is that logical?

- What would you tell the activists against bilingual education if you had a positive experience in a bilingual class?

Perhaps you could become an activist yourself, joining your parents after careful consideration of where you stand.

You might think about how America has traditionally tolerated language differences.

For example, in the state of Hawaii both English and Hawaiian are spoken. When you drive north from Boston you encounter big signs reading "Welcome to New Hampshire" *and* "Bienvenu à New Hampshire" (in French). If it's okay to have bilingual signs for drivers, do you think it's all right to teach in two languages in schools?

Gabriela

Gabriela came to the United States from Mexico during sixth grade. She knew only a few words of English.

On the first day of school, she was afraid. Everybody talked so fast and in a language she couldn't understand. In the school office she begged her mother to let her go home.

"No, *mi hija*" (no, my daughter), her mother answered, and explained how important education would be for her future. "Don't worry," she continued, "you'll learn English in no time."

Because Gabriela had several classmates from Mexico and San Salvador, and because she spoke only Spanish at home, it took her almost a full school year to speak English fairly well.

In the meantime, however, she had fallen behind in math, in reading, and in history because she had trouble understanding the teacher.

The issue of bilingualism has two types of activists at work. Mostly, U.S. citizens believe that children who come to this country should learn the language through immersion, which means that only English is spoken in schools.

The other type of activist demands that teachers be hired who speak Spanish or Korean or whatever language is needed by many students in a particular school. They argue that this will prevent the students from falling behind as Gabriela did.

What Would You Say If . . .

You attend a school where lessons are taught in two languages, but your activist parents are against it and believe in immersion?

- Can you put yourself in the place of the boy or girl who cannot understand you?
- Can you see how embarrassing it might be if you laughed with a friend while a Spanish-speaking student near you thought you were laughing at him?

Yet your mother is working very hard for a program of immersion.

"I came to the United States when I was twelve years old," she tells you. "At that time bilingual education wasn't even thought of. So I had to pay close attention in order to learn English."

"That's right," your father chimes in. "When I moved to Israel for five years, I was put in an immersion program for six weeks to learn enough Hebrew to get by."

Your parents want summer camps for foreign-speaking

students in which only English would be spoken. They are convinced that American teachers should not have to learn another language in order to teach. They are activists for immersion.

You remember Gabriela and want the best for her. You recall the student who couldn't understand your laughter.

- Do you agree with your parents about programs of immersion?

What would you say if your parents were activists for bilingualism not only in schools, but on the radio, on TV, on billboards, and in grocery stores.

Your parents are world travelers and have noticed how many people in other countries speak English but how few Americans speak other languages.

They believe that bilingualism would enrich Americans and make them more aware of other cultures.

You recall Gabriela and how she fell behind in her studies. Would she have done better in a bilingual setting?

You think about the student who couldn't laugh with you and your friend. Had someone translated your joke, would he have felt more a part of your group?

- If you disagree with your parents' point of view, be sure you have enough facts to back up your argument. You are entitled to your belief, whether it is immersion or bilingualism.
- In which situation do you think a young adult would feel more comfortable and have greater self-esteem?
- Have you ever felt like a stranger in any situation? Did someone help you out?

• How would you react if you became friends with a Spanish-speaking student and were invited to his home where only Spanish was spoken?

Laws regarding bilingualism have been made in many states. These laws have come into being thanks to activists.

It all comes down to one thing—unity. How can you promote it if you agree with your parents' activism?

Once again, this issue need not be an either/or one. You can have both negative and positive feelings. When you handle disagreements with your parents' activism with mutual respect, you will benefit and learn a great deal.

PART ◇ III

SUCCESSFUL AND UNSUCCESSFUL COPING STRATEGIES

CHAPTER 8

How Do You Know If You Have a Problem?

T he very fact that you are reading this book about coping with your parents' activism tells you that you have concerns and questions. At times you may feel uneasy about the emotional way in which your parents talk about their chosen cause.

Moreover, you may be embarrassed if your parents talk to your friends about their activism and try to convince them of the value of their work.

You may even say to yourself, "Why do they stick their noses in other people's business. Isn't that what our government is for?" or "Why don't they just leave me alone about all that stuff? They should be more interested in their children."

When you have these thoughts, do you realize that you want to tell them what to do? In a sense you want to interfere in their lives.

Do you have a "bill of rights" in your family? Of course,

it is an unspoken one. Take a look at your parents, brothers, and sisters.

Let's begin with your parents, since you feel uncomfortable about their activism. Here are some questions to think about:

1. Before they joined their cause, do you think you got more attention?
2. How old were you when you were more satisfied with the amount of time you spent with your mother or father?
3. Was there ever a time when you wanted them to leave you alone to solve your own problems? How old were you then?
4. In your imaginary "bill of rights" what can you realistically expect from your parents as a teenager?
5. What can you not expect from your parents at this point? Is *expect* a good word?

You probably noticed in answering the questions that you got more attention when you were younger. There were still many things you couldn't do for yourself. Moreover, your decision-making skills were not as sharp as they are now. You needed Mom and Dad to help you every day with one thing or another, from getting dressed, to homework, to sports or music lessons.

As you grew older, their attention may have annoyed you at times. You may have acted as though your parents didn't realize you were growing up. And—you may have been right. Constant hovering by Mom or constant advice from Dad made your temper flare.

Perhaps they realized their mistake. Your brothers

and sisters were growing, too, and were able to do most things for themselves.

Your parents might have felt a need for themselves. They liked taking care of the family, but they were no longer as essential as they once had been.

So they threw themselves into a cause and became activists in something they had always believed in. Their activism was two-pronged: On one hand they allowed you and your siblings to become more independent, and on the other hand they satisfied their own need to give to others.

Now you are somewhat confused. How much can you still want from them? After all, you declared your wish to be left more and more alone. You realize, however, that you still have a need for your parents. You want to plan your future—college, career. You need to talk to them about a teacher with whom you have trouble or a subject that is hard for you. You'd like to speak to them about your girlfriend or boyfriend. You want to know about sex, about AIDS, even about such small matters as your complexion, which isn't always the greatest.

Does your "bill of rights" demand that your parents be available for your problems? If you answer yes, you are right. No doubt, your folks would be delighted to know that you still need them in some ways—perhaps not daily, but definitely from time to time.

If you approach them with a positive attitude, and not just as they are walking out the door, you will undoubtedly receive from them what you need.

However, you cannot "expect" your parents to be mind readers. You have to talk about your problems and concerns.

You also cannot "expect" your parents to give up their activism. It is important to them to contribute something to society. Don't try to take it away from them. Remember, in your "bill of rights" your parents require the freedom to make decisions, too.

Terry at Seventeen

Terry was deaf from birth. At first her parents were devastated. How would they communicate with their child?

They took her from one doctor to another to see if an operation could enable her to hear. However, Terry had nerve damage, so nothing could be done.

None of the doctors considered it a major tragedy, because they knew Terry could learn sign language as well as lipreading.

"But we'll have to learn it, too," her parents complained. They felt insecure about their ability to cope.

When they took Terry to a clinic and later to a nursery school for the deaf and hard-of-hearing, they were amazed how fast their baby learned to "talk" by signing. Her mother and father sometimes lagged behind, but by the time she was ready for kindergarten the family "talked" all the time.

When Terry went to high school, she was placed in a deaf program but mainstreamed into regular classes for two hours each day.

She was able to lipread perfectly, and she could speak, though in a hollow voice.

Some of the students laughed when she spoke, and she decided then and there to become an activist in her school.

She went to the principal and requested that her history class attend a few sessions in her deaf and hard-of-hearing classes. The principal was happy to arrange it. The hearing students were impressed and no longer laughed.

Terry began to write a column about deaf people for the school paper and started a support group with an advisor. Her program spread to other schools in town.

Her parents realized what a special daughter they had. They asked if they could contribute anything, and Terry was delighted.

Now her parents work and lobby for more main-streaming of deaf and hard-of-hearing students. They also are activists in educating the hearing population to appreciate and give jobs to deaf people. They make speeches, write pamphlets, and are happily involved with their daughter and her friends and coworkers.

- Did Terry expect anything from her parents when she first began her activism?
- Why do you think Terry's parents changed their attitude of despair about their daughter's deafness to one of pride?
- If Terry's parents had not become involved and expanded her activities, do you think Terry would have been angry?
- How does this family's "bill of rights" work to allow everyone independence?

How Much Should Your Parents "Expect" of You?

When babies are born most parents give them uncon-ditional love. That means that the infant is fully accepted. There is no criticism about anything. Although uncondi-tional love is simple, it is very hard to teach to people who themselves have never experienced it.

Conditional love, on the other hand, has barriers. For

example, your mother or father may act as though to say, "I will love you if you will do something for me."

If your parents want good behavior, that doesn't mean they don't love you unconditionally. They may also want you to *try* your best in various endeavors.

However, if the inner message you get from your parents is, "Be interested and involved in things we are interested in," they are putting a condition on their love.

If they try to force you into some form of activism at the expense of your interests, that is an expectation that goes beyond the boundaries of love.

Keep in mind that you are primary for yourself. In other words, love yourself and be gentle to yourself.

Mitchell's Dad

Mitchell's father was a successful businessman. Each year he made more and more money. But each year, too, he began to drink more and more as the stress of his work deepened.

Mitchell's mother was horrified when she found her husband drinking beer for breakfast and escalating to Scotch in the afternoon and brandy at night.

Mitchell heard his parents fighting constantly. His father in his drunkenness would grant any wish of Mitchell's, while his mother attempted to persuade him that their son needed discipline.

One day Mitchell's dad bought him an expensive sports car. Mitchell was thrilled, and he drove the powerful car up and down city streets ignoring traffic signals. He thought wearing seat belts was "sissy stuff."

What happened? You guessed it. There was an accident. But it was Dad behind the wheel, with Mitchell in the passenger seat. Both were drunk. Because Mitchell adored his father, he followed his footsteps in drinking. He paid no attention to the other part, which was hard work in the business world.

Mitchell's mother, unable to persuade her husband to change, joined MADD (Mothers Against Drunk Driving). She became an activist and *expected* Mitchell to come to his senses and work with her in an attempt to stop drunk driving.

"If you love me, you'll do this," she often said to Mitchell. Was she showing unconditional love?

Mitchell was torn between his father's "fun-loving" ways and his mother's sober expectations.

Each of these parents "expected" something that did not represent unconditional love. Mitchell did not join his mother's activism, nor did he want to drive the car any longer.

When parents expect something unrealistic of you, you probably feel angry. Who is right? Underneath your anger you may experience fear. After all, you're not an adult yet, and your parents are pulling at you from opposite sides.

If you are in a situation such as Mitchell's, don't deny what is really going on. If you fail to make a decision and remain passive, everything will stay inside of you and your problems will grow.

Become your own parent and friend: Make a decision.

- How could Mitchell's mother have persuaded him to help in her activism without *expecting* it?
- Do you think Mitchell's father could have been helped when he saw how he was hurting his family?

- Even if the father's drinking problem was not solved, how could the activism of mother and son have helped others?
- Are we responsible for others' behavior? Do you think MADD does worthwhile work in trying to prevent deaths through traffic accidents?
- Did Mitchell's father have the right to expect him to follow in his footsteps?

Expectations must not have a "should" in front of them. Even the word *expect* often leads to disappointment.

- You *should* do your homework right after school.
- Parents *should* *expect* their children to love them.
- You *should* be *expected* to follow in your parents' footsteps.

Suppose we take the words *expect* and *should* out of our vocabulary for the moment, and substitute *responsibility* and *reliability* instead. Let's change Mitchell's story.

Mitchell's parents were extremely successful business people. When they arrived home from work, Mitchell's mother was keyed up and told her son stories about what had happened during the day. She also asked Mitchell how his day had passed, and listened.

His father was completely stressed by business and generally made his way to the liquor cabinet, having three or four drinks "to relax."

Mitchell worried and asked his mother about his dad's obvious problem.

"As long as he stays home it's all right, I guess," she answered distractedly.

Now Mitchell was sure there was a problem, because his mother was usually forthright. He realized that she did not want to worry him.

One day his father decided that he could work at home four days a week. He installed a few telephones, a computer, and a modem in the den. Moreover, he bought a liquor cabinet for his new "office" in case, he said, other businessmen visited him.

On his way to school a month later, Mitchell saw his father drinking beer at 7:30 in the morning.

That afternoon when he came home, Dad had graduated to Scotch. Mitchell was upset and decided to take matters into his own hands.

He entered the office and confronted his father. The answer, "Son, I've taken care of myself and this family for years. I was waiting for a client and just wanted to look relaxed." Mitchell decided to ask his mother the next day what could be done.

However, when he came home from school the next day a new red sports car was parked in front of the house. On the windshield was a sign: "For Mitchell, Who Worries About His Dad." He ran inside and hugged his father, who smelled of alcohol and had a little trouble standing up.

"Dad," Mitch said, "thank you so much for the beautiful car," and in the same breath, "You've been drinking again."

"Don't be silly," his father slurred, "let's go for a spin. I'll drive."

"No, Dad—you're drunk."

"Come with me, son," his father growled.

"Only if I can drive."

"No way! I bought the car and I wanna show you how fast it goes."

With that, his father lurched to the car and drove off by himself to the tune of screeching tires.

The police called an hour later. Mitchell's father had gotten into an accident and had hit a child. The child was in the hospital with a broken leg and multiple contusions—but alive.

Mitchell's father was at the police station waiting to be picked up. No amount of talking changed him. He continued to drink and miraculously continued being a successful businessman.

Mitchell's mother became an activist in MADD. As usual, in the evening mother and son talked about their days. Now there was a new topic: Mother's activism in MADD. She didn't ask Mitchell to join her, but he became so interested that he asked if he could help with typing, news releases, or anything the organization needed. His mother was thrilled, and he became a working member. She had not put a condition on her love. Mitchell felt free to make a choice.

- Does anyone have the right to *expect* anything of anyone?
- Can there be unconditional love in an atmosphere of *should's, have to's* and *expectations*?
- A good example by a parent is an important part of showing unconditional love. If you are growing up in such a home, what can you do to show your love? Can you accept your parent as you are being accepted?
- Do you suppose Mitchell and his mother grew even closer during their activist work? Why?

Keeping a Journal

If you live in a home where someone is always coming or going and no one has time to listen to you, keep a journal.

A journal is similar to a diary, but it is a real document in which you can record times you wanted to talk to your mother or father and how you felt at the time. Also, write down how much they are at home and what they do when they remain there.

Sometimes activism can take up too much time and detract from the family.

At other times, however, you may only think that your parents are never there. Your journal will tell you the truth. They may be around more than you give them credit for; *you* may be the busy one when they have time for you.

A journal is a useful tool, not only if you are upset about your parents' activism, but to give you insights just for yourself.

CHAPTER 9

Unsuccessful Coping Strategies

I t is almost time for an important state election. Both of your parents are deeply involved in the campaign. There are papers, slogans, hats, pins, and what not all over the living room. The phone rings constantly—and it is not for you.

You're failing in chemistry, and your father is a chemist.

"Dad," you call out to him, "I need help."

"In what, son?" Dad answers, but he doesn't look at you. He is setting up chairs in the living room for a political meeting.

"Chemistry; I'm failing," you shout.

"You're failing in a subject? Talk to me later. We'll get a tutor."

"I'M FAILING IN CHEMISTRY," you scream.

Now your father is angry. You have his full attention, but it is not the kind of attention you want.

"Don't ever scream at me again, young man," he says. "When you calm down you may talk to me."

"You haven't heard a word I said," you answer through clenched teeth. "Fine. I'm leaving before all your creeps arrive."

Your father stands in the living room holding a sheaf of papers. He is not used to such behavior.

You put on your jacket and slam the door as you go out. A second later, you open it and call sarcastically, "Hey, Dad. Don't count on Princeton. I'll probably flunk out of a community college." You slam the door again, for effect.

That kind of rebellion is not a successful way of handling your busy parent. You are angry, your dad is angry, and even worse, you feel lost and worthless. Your self-esteem is suffering.

- How could you have handled the situation differently?
- Did you approach your Dad at a good time?
- If you had kept a journal, what might you have written about failing in chemistry, especially since your father is a chemist?
- How might you have felt once you left the house and found yourself out in the street?

Avoidance

You already know that keeping your emotions bottled up is dangerous. You are bound to explode, not knowing where to express your anger.

One way of keeping your emotions caged is by avoidance—acting as though nothing really bothers you.

Suppose your mother is an activist in a Neighborhood Watch program. Perhaps many of your friends' parents attend meetings at which your mother is the chairperson. Sometimes she has speakers from the police, or psychologists, to discuss fear. Many of the meetings are held in your home.

You think all this hullabaloo is unnecessary. After all, you tell yourself, they could buy a security system. Why do all these parents have to gawk at me whenever they come over?

So you decide not to be at home after the first few meetings. You go to the library or to a movie and stew about it. You'd rather be at home watching your favorite TV show or doing your homework without twenty or thirty people heatedly expressing themselves about protecting their homes.

At the first meeting at your house, you heard a woman say, "It's today's kids. They're the ones who break in to get money for dope."

You wanted to tell her what you thought of that falsehood. But it wasn't your meeting. The worst part was that several voices agreed with the speaker! And some of those voices belonged to parents of your classmates.

You wondered if these people even remotely knew their sons and daughters. Your friends are hard-working students, eager to go to college in a year or two. How could these parents even suggest that a Neighborhood Watch was necessary because of "those kids."

Of course, you didn't tell your mother or father how you felt. You simply avoided the whole issue by going out whenever a group of activists appeared at your home.

You kept quiet, occasionally throwing a sidelong glance at your mother. "Is it possible," you'd ask yourself, "that she thinks I could steal from someone's home? Is that why she's so involved in the Neighborhood Watch?"

Your avoidance kept on growing. Soon you didn't want

to go out with the family, because you weren't sure how they perceived you.

If something else bothered you, you kept the problem to yourself. You became angry and sullen. No one in the family could approach you, and you gave only minimal answers to questions.

Your anger had nowhere to go. It just grew and grew.

- What could you have done right from the beginning of the Neighborhood Watch program?
- How many people actually accused kids of being the perpetrators of crimes?
- What do you think was really the beginning of your unsuccessful coping strategy with your activist parent?
- What might have happened had you talked out your frustration after the first meeting?
- Why were you upset that your classmates' parents came to your home? Did you feel shy, out of place, embarrassed, angry? Look into yourself, and talk with your friends about it. After all, it was sometimes their folks' turn to hold a meeting. How did *they* feel?

Neighborhood Watch programs have been fairly successful all over the country. Your mother was probably trying to protect the family, but you were looking at it with an attitude of avoidance that progressed to anger. You can successfully cope with your mother's activism by trying to understand the reason for it and seeing the person who spoke out against kids for what she was— insensitive and prejudiced.

Stating how you feel is a wonderful release—and you can do it.

Moreover, since you knew that neither you nor your friends would ever steal, there must have been another reason for the Neighborhood Watch program. Can you think of several?

Avoidance is a way of not facing the truth about a situation. Don't let it overcome you. Meet it head-on and find out what you need to know in order to cope.

Playing One Parent Against the Other

One of the oldest tricks children practice is playing one parent against the other.

Have you ever asked a friend to go to a movie? Your friend may have said she had to ask her parents first.

She asked her mother if she could go with you on Saturday afternoon, but the reply was a firm no. It seemed that the family had previous plans.

So your friend asked her father. As he came home from work and was taking off his coat, she said, "Dad, may I please go to a movie Saturday afternoon?"

Her dad was tired and only half listened. "Of course, you may," he responded absent-mindedly.

Naturally, your friend's devious plan of playing one parent against the other came out.

"I told her she couldn't go," the mother explained heatedly to her husband.

"What's the harm in a movie?" the father retorted.

That really wasn't the issue, was it? To get her way, your friend caused a problem between her parents. That sort of behavior can go on in different situations, as well.

Nancy's Private War

Nancy's parents and her twin brothers were very much involved in environmental issues. All of them were activists who realized that something had to be done to save the earth for future generations. They believed they had to give something back because their lives were good. The parents tried to raise their children with social consciences.

They nearly succeeded. Only Nancy was adamant in her refusal to participate. "I'm too young to worry about the next generation," she'd argue. "I *am* the next generation."

Whenever she was asked to come along to plant trees, or to hear a speech about the dangers of smog or the hole in the ozone layer, she'd find an excuse. Her parents and her brothers couldn't understand her attitude.

One day in history class Nancy read about the British conquest of India. India had been ruled by many maharajas who all had separate kingdoms. The British used a method called "divide and conquer" to seize the whole country and place it under their rule. What it meant was pitting one kingdom against another. Enmity and wars followed, and India became weak through the insidious division of the kingdoms. The British won!

That gave Nancy an idea. She would divide her family and get out of the environmental activism they wanted her to participate in.

Nancy began a long campaign with her mother about her need to study. She explained that she had to concentrate more than some other students to get good grades. Her mother, impressed with her daughter's dedication to schoolwork, excused her lack of interest in making the world a better place.

When Nancy's father and brothers objected, her mother became an advocate for Nancy's "studious behavior."

"We go to school, too," the twins said, "but we make time to help out. Why can't she?"

Nancy knew that she had successfully divided her family and her conquest was clear. She didn't have to help because she had convinced her mother of her need to concentrate more than others in school.

She had set her mother against her father and brothers.

- Unsuccessful coping strategies often use unfair methods. What method did Nancy use?
- If she was uninterested in the family's activism, how could she have handled the situation without using a "divide and conquer" strategy?

In the long run, Nancy's strategy with her family failed. She got what she thought she wanted, but while her brothers and parents grew by giving and by appreciating our beautiful world, Nancy was left with just Nancy.

- Was she really a winner, or did she lose out on something important?

CHAPTER 10

Successful Coping
Strategies

There are times when you can appreciate and admire your parents' activism without participating in it.

For example, a group called Action for Children's Television (ACT) became a powerful force. If your parents were in it, you as a youngster could give them more than emotional support.

The group dissolved recently after working together for twenty-three years. Peggy Charren, an influential advocate of better TV programs for young people, says that Action for Children's Television had accomplished its goal with passage by Congress of the Children's Television Act. Now, she says, it's up to the public to keep the pressure on.

If your parents were in this activist group, their success in getting a law passed for your welfare and that of other youngsters might make you admire them. You know how many programs are violent and hateful, how many have unbelievably crude commercials. ACT got Congress to say to the Federal Communications Commission, "You have to provide programs specifically designed to meet the education and information needs of children as a condition of license renewal."

If your parents helped Peggy Charren, the main advocate, you could have acknowledged their attempts and their success. You might have told your class about it during oral language time. Other students might then have discussed with their teacher having interesting TV programs that didn't involve constant killing, automobile crashes, and mindless conversation.

A full page in *Time* magazine (January 20, 1992) was devoted to Peggy Charren and ACT. Their concern was more than the programming; they opposed the manipulation of kids by sponsors promoting junk foods and toys.

If you thank your parents for "Afternoon Specials" and "30 Minutes," the newsmagazine for kids, your parents will feel their work has been worthwhile. Although they participated not only for you, but for all young people your age, your appreciation of their hard work is the icing on the cake. You performed a successful coping strategy.

Another successful coping strategy might be helping around the house to free your parents for their activist work. You might volunteer to baby-sit younger brothers and sisters and tell your parents you are doing it because they are teaching you a valuable lesson in social consciousness. Giving back to others for our good fortune is a positive step. If you recognize it, don't hesitate to praise your parents. They will appreciate it and go to their activist meetings with a sense of peace. You are giving much-needed emotional support without becoming a mini-activist yourself.

Sometimes the shoe is on the other foot, and the activist is the son or daughter.

Aaron Gordon

Aaron took a school bus to go to a science museum from Miami's Leewood Elementary School. At that time he was only in second grade.

Suddenly the bus lurched forward and stopped short. Students were jolted out of their seats.

Aaron wondered why no one had a seat belt.

More than 6,000 students are hurt in school bus accidents yearly, but the National Transportation Safety Board doesn't like standard lap belts for children because they can cause internal injuries.

Aaron, now ten years old, wondered why shoulder harnesses couldn't be used. He became an activist and got 4,000 signatures to show the Dade County School Board that the community supported his idea.

The board was impressed and admitted that Aaron knew more about it than they did.

His mother encouraged him.

When the board learned that it would cost up to $5,000 for each bus, they vetoed Aaron's idea.

What did Aaron do? He wrote to Florida's Commissioner of Education. But she only sent him some information about lap belts.

When Aaron took a plane trip a few weeks later, he noticed that the flight attendants wore shoulder-straps during take-off and landing.

With the help of his mother, a teacher, and his father, a lawyer, Aaron phoned State Representative Dory Jones of South Dade County and—got an appointment. Mr. Jones got the legislature to allocate $25,000 for research.

Now the center for Urban Transportation Research in Tampa has started work on a new shoulder restraint similar to Aaron's suggestion. If the restraint works, Aaron's name will be on the patent.

Of course, kids would have to be reminded about wearing the new seat belts.

Aaron has an answer for that, too. "People with a certain number of speeding tickets, or if they were, like, drunk driving, would have to be monitors on the school bus." Aaron is only ten years old.*

Why, you may ask, is this story part of good coping strategies with activist parents? The answer is simple: It is the other side of the same coin. The activist in the family was the son, but the parents encouraged him and lent him moral support over a period of years. And it worked!

Similarly, you can help make your parents' activism successful through cheering them on and above all lending them emotional support.

Hidden Agendas

There are times when a parent becomes an activist not so much because of a social conscience as to forget something painful while being busy with a cause.

Let's look at some examples.

Joe's Death

Your older brother, Joe, was the pride of the family and your hero. Not only was he a football star in high school,

*People, 1992.

but his grades were fantastic. On top of it all, he was kind and always had time to help anyone who needed it. It seemed to you that everyone smiled in Joe's presence.

Suddenly, he didn't have the energy he usually exhibited. He looked pale, and although he never complained, he slept more and seemed to have lots of discomfort.

The football coach told him to take a break, maybe go to the doctor and get some vitamins.

After Joe's visit to the doctor, the diagnosis was grim: He had leukemia. A few short months later, he died.

Needless to say, everyone who had known Joe was devastated. In particular, your mother acted as though she had little to live for. She got up late, lost interest in the house, gave up her job, and constantly apologized for her listless behavior.

One day a friend came to visit her. Instead of consoling or condoling, she told your mother to *do* something. She insisted that your mother go with her to an antidrug meeting. She said it was to help teenagers of Joe's age, as well as drug-addicted parents.

Your mother only half listened, but she did go with her friend, and she learned some shocking facts. She discovered that in every year since 1975 more than 90 per cent of high school seniors had tried alcohol and over 50 percent had used an illegal drug. Your mother began, slowly at first, then more and more, to work with Narcotics Anonymous. The need she had to love her son was partially fulfilled when she saw how much she was needed by drug abusers.

You were amazed at the change in your mother as her deep grief slowly turned to activism, but you knew why she had become an activist. Her hidden agenda was to move into life again after the death of her son.

There may have been times after the death of a family member when you felt you weren't enough for your mother. However, since you also felt grief, was your mother enough for you?

If you give that question some thought you will find that losing someone does not mean you have to become more than you are to be "enough." A period of grief is normal.

Joe's mother's activism partially solved the problem of her loneliness and paved a road back to the family. Her usefulness in the drug program raised her self-esteem. She was now able to be more herself again.

There are, of course, other problems, other reasons for hidden agendas.

Your father may not feel secure or appreciated in his job and turn to activism in a good cause. There he is told how wonderful his work is. He may even become a leader of a group.

However, the primary reason for his activism is to make up for the pain he feels at his job.

Look at your father with compassion. Do you think he's a phony for spending many hours in activist work? Before you answer, try to look back on a bad day at school. You didn't have your math homework finished, your term paper didn't interest you, and your team lost the basketball game. How did you feel? Suppose someone had come up to you and asked, "Could you help me study for my history test? I know you're a whiz at it." You may have decided to help your friend. You were no longer the loser you felt all day. You had a friend who admired your skill.

Your father's hidden agenda is also to feel worthwhile, to have a sense of importance and of self-esteem, because he is not appreciated at work.

- In these two stories, do you think a hidden agenda is dishonest?
- If a hidden agenda helps a person, _____ _____ (finish the sentence).

Hidden Agendas in Solving Family Problems

Some family problems give rise to hidden agendas. If someone wants to escape a dysfunctional family and turns to a group of people who are activists, the hidden agenda is not being addressed; it is not spoken about or brought out in the open.

The Nelson Family

Mike Nelson was a plumber, and every day when he returned home to his wife and seven children, there was noise and chaos in the house.

Upstairs, Mike Jr. played his stereo loud enough to burst one's eardrums. The two youngest fought over a toy. His twelve-year-old daughter laughed hysterically on the phone. His wife shouted to his sons about chores not done. No one acknowledged Mr. Nelson's presence as he entered the kitchen, where last night's stew was being heated up.

Mike Nelson wanted to turn around and run away. He envied his fellow workers who told him about their quiet homes or described a restaurant where they had gone to dinner the night before.

Mike seldom talked. His children avoided him, and his wife had a daily list of complaints. One night Mike could take no more. "Nothing here is appreciated," he shouted. The family was shocked. He'd never raised his voice before. "You have a roof over your heads, clothes on your backs, and food on the table."

"That isn't enough," his oldest son shouted.

"Everybody always fights. I can't even ask my girl-friends to visit," Mike's daughter screamed.

"At least you're not homeless!" Mike was now beside himself. "Every day as I come home I see decent men and women on the street who've lost their livelihood." An uncomfortable silence followed, but no one tried to understand anyone else, least of all Mr. Nelson.

The following week Mike Nelson came home very late. He had gone to his veterans organization and discovered that many veterans were homeless. He thought, "I might as well help my buddies and also get a little appreciation." As he began to get involved, he noticed how vulnerable the homeless felt and realized that anyone could end up like that. He found out that the homeless are veterans, the elderly, children, whole families, and the mentally ill. He devoted many hours a week talking to them and working with his organization to supply food and find shelter.

Mike worked quietly and efficiently. He never told his family about his "extra job," nor did they ask. They had ignored him for too long.

Mike's hidden agenda was to find a place where he would be appreciated, even loved.

He did not address the problem that plagued his family: They did not function as a group.

- How could Mike have gotten his family to listen to him?
- What did everyone in the family need?
- Although he worked well with the homeless, how might Mike's hidden agenda ultimately have hurt the family even more?
- If you had been one of Mike's sons or daughters,

what coping mechanisms could you have used to uncover your father's hidden agenda and bring it out in the open?

Finding Common Values

The most desirable activism, combined with a good family life, is having common values.

If your parents share such values as loyalty, altruism (helping others), and honesty, they will pass these on to you through their actions. If your parents are people you trust and can depend on, chances are excellent that you, too, will become a trustworthy, dependable person. It would hardly be a surprise to you if your parents told you they were interested in joining an activist cause. Chances are that they would discuss it with you, actually consult with you beforehand. That would make you feel part of them, help you to understand them, and allow you to give them emotional support.

It might interest you to know that in a recent national study 84 percent of Americans agreed that "at middle age, a person becomes more compassionate."

Once children are grown, nurturing feelings go on and can broaden beyond the family, according to Monsignor Charles J. Fahey, Director of Fordham University's Third Age Center.* There is a strong potential for greater involvement with community and social issues.

If your parents take you into their confidence and explain the issues of their activism, it will make it easy for you to cope with them.

Their values have been taught to you by example, and

* *Reader's Digest*, October 1991.

you may share them and feel pride in your mother's and father's selfless tasks.

Some Practical Steps

All coping begins with yourself. First and foremost do a self-examination.

1. Are you really pleased about your parents' activism?
2. Does the cause they chose embarrass you? If so, is it intrinsic (inside yourself) or extrinsic (worry about what others may say)?
3. Are you jealous of their time away from you?
4. Are you angry that the phone is always ringing— for them; not for you.

If you answered these questions honestly and have come to the conclusion that you neither agree with nor understand your folks, *talk* with your family.

You saw in the example of shared common values how easy it is to feel part of the enthusiasm of an activist family.

If everyone is closed in, however, understanding is difficult, and misunderstanding is easy.

Discuss your problem with friends and counselors. Become better informed about the issues of activism, the reasons for it, and your feelings about it. In that way you have a better meeting of minds and cooperation within your family unit.

Keeping anger or frustration inside is not coping. It is rather a way of letting a problem grow—a problem that might be solved by talking it out and by being interested in the issues.

You can call a family meeting, because you are an important member of this primary group.

If you discover that your mother or father uses activism as a hidden agenda, perhaps you can point it out gently and through your compassion and thoughtfulness gain the respect of your parents. They may still engage in activism, but they, like you, will have an understanding of their reasons.

Most activists operate out of a desire to do the right thing, to give back to society for the rights and privileges they receive from it. With such values before you, not only will you be able to cope with your activist parents, but your interest may be piqued so that you, too, will one day give selflessly to a cause.

PART IV

OVERVIEW OF TYPES OF ACTIVISM

CHAPTER ◇ 11

The Environmental

Activist

Environmental activists work to solve the garbage crisis, to save tropical rain forests, to stabilize the world population, to protect our coasts, and to keep the Great Lakes clean, among other things.

It's a big job, and of course, no one is involved in all of those causes.

One group may, for example, investigate companies that damage the environment and decide to lobby the state legislature to make them clean up their pollution.

When an important environmental bill is pending in Congress and several legislators are still undecided, the environmental activist gets to work, flooding Capitol Hill with letters and phone calls that make a difference.

You can help out, as well. Whenever you turn on the lights, dump the garbage, or drive from one place to another, you impact the environment. For example, when you walk or bicycle instead of driving, you not only reduce the pollution and the build-up of greenhouse gases but lessen the pressure to drill for oil in ecologically sensitive areas.

Your parents want a safe world for you to grow up in. Their activism just may be for you and generations to come.

Your mother may use an integrated approach to diet, food preparation, and kitchen design as well as kitchen gardening. She may teach members of her group and friends a safer method of working with food. She, too, is an activist.

The Sierra Club is well known. They work on hundreds of conservation issues. They are politically active by finding out how congressional representatives voted on key pieces of environmental legislation.

There is much more to know, but at least you can be aware of the interests of your environmentally activist parents.

Surprise them with your knowledge, ask questions, and they in turn will probably have a spirited and warm-hearted time with you.

CHAPTER 12

The Gay Activist

In a particularly difficult sixth-grade class in Los Angeles, the teacher called in the school psychologist to see what could be done. The students fought a great deal, resisted learning, and littered the classroom floor with obscene notes.

For the first few days, amid much grumbling, the teacher had the children move their desks against the wall. Then they placed their chairs in a circle so they could see each other and no one could whisper nasty comments without everyone's noticing it. The psychologist came to the class daily for an hour, and he and the teacher sat in the circle with the students.

At first the discussions were very superficial: "He hit me in the playground." "She pulled my hair in the bathroom." "Everybody always copies my papers." No one was criticized for their comments.

By the end of the second week trust had been established between the class and the teacher and psychologist. Many students told their problems honestly.

One boy, Fred, never contributed a word, however. He sat in his chair cracking his knuckles and shifting from one side to the other, at times even turning his back to the group.

On Monday of the third week the psychologist asked Fred please to face the group.

"I know what you want," Fred shouted, his face getting red. "You probably read my school records. My mother is an attorney, okay? She works for NOW [National Organization for Women], okay? Everybody on our block knows she's an activist for the Lesbian Task Force."

"What's that?" a girl asked.

"What's that?" Fred snarled. "It just wrecks my life, that's all. She's gay, she's a lesbian, she divorced my dad and lives with this woman. All these gay guys and women come to our house for meetings. How do you think I feel?" It had all come out in a torrent of words.

The students were quiet. Fred sat back and cracked his knuckles.

Suddenly, the boisterous team captain spoke up, "Hey, Fred, we get to play softball today. Want to bat first?"

Fred began to cry. Students jumped out of their seats, to the surprise of the teacher and the psychologist.

"It's not your fault," one of the children said.

"We're sorry we've been mean," another chimed in.

"How did it happen?" a thoughtful girl wondered.

The class asked the teacher about gay life and why anybody would want to be an activist for that group. They were interested and began to form a more cohesive group. They decided to learn something about gay activism and about other problems the students had brought up. These are some of the things they discovered.

Gay men and women simply love people of the same sex. Often they live together much as married people do, buying homes, adopting children, and leading quiet lives. The AIDS scare came along, however, and changed everything. A new disease called the acquired immuno-deficiency syndrome was discovered, and it was found to be fatal to anyone who contracted it. When at first it seemed limited to gay men and people who shared needles to use intravenous drugs, the gay community became an object of hatred and fear.

Later it was found that AIDS can infect almost anyone, including children, but by that time gays had been identified with the disease. Children with AIDS were not allowed to go to school because people thought they could infect other students. That is not true, and *activists* worked to ensure that children with the disease could attend classes.

Other activists are working toward allowing gays to marry. Some churches have a marriage ceremony for gays, but the relationship is not recognized by law. What activists want is to give gays the right to will property to the child of a gay couple and to care for the child if one of the parents dies. The activists believe that a homosexual couple should have the same rights as a heterosexual couple. (When Fred found all this out, he relaxed quite a bit.)

Still, a great deal of help is needed with the AIDS crisis. Ignorance has fostered prejudice and insensitivity toward adults and children with the disease. Myths about gays not only encourage discrimination and fear, but they hide the real causes for the spread of the virus.

That is why friends, family members, and volunteers are so essential. Education, prevention, and understanding can combat the gay rights issue and the hysteria that has accompanied it.

Caring people like Fred's mother and her activist friends help to provide support and much-needed compassion.

- Do you think Fred felt better when the whole class sympathized with him?
- What was more important, sympathy or an understanding of the problem?
- What might have happened to the relationship between Fred and his mother after he learned about the issues?

One of the worst things going on now is "gay bashing," men who look for homosexuals and beat them up, sometimes even killing them.

One young man was asked by a news reporter why he liked to hurt gays.

"They're just not human, that's all," he responded.

Do you think activists could help keep peaceful gays safe?

Another problem recently faced by gays is with the Boy Scouts of America. One troop decided to accept gay Scout Masters as well as gay boys. Because of that, the organization wants to oust the troop entirely. Already activists are working on the issue. The story has been aired on television, and perhaps it will be possible to help the troop achieve a fair decision.

(Fred's sixth-grade class was stunned, and some of them even asked their heterosexual parents to become activists.)

CHAPTER 13

The Animal Rights Activist

I f you have considered your activist parent overly concerned in his work for animal rights, the following facts may shock you.

1. The number of animals that suffer and are killed in this country is unbelievable. According to the World Society for the Protection of Animals, more than one hundred million animals are killed every year for their fur alone.
2. Of fifty million animals caught each year in "instant-kill" devices, thirty million have been the wrong animals. The traps have caught cats, dogs, and endangered species.
3. The International Society for Animal Rights estimates that more than fifteen million animals suffer and die each year in tests to decide the safety of cosmetics and household products.
4. According to Friends of Animals, animal shelters

all over the nation euthanize (put to sleep, kill) as many as eighteen million dogs and cats each year, many of which had been neglected or abandoned by their owners. In many states, pound animals are used for laboratory experiments.

5. The National Audubon Society estimates that 11,000 endangered sea turtles drown in shrimp fishing nets every year.

There are many more horror stories about endangered species.

Perhaps you can understand why animal rights activism has become an important issue. On one side the belief is that animals deserve equal protection under the law, that cruelty to them is no different from cruelty to people. On the other side the belief is that people can use animals for their own purposes.

Think about these questions:

- Is using animals in medical research acceptable under any circumstances, only in certain cases, or not at all?
- If a person refuses to eat meat, should milk and eggs be avoided as well?
- Is fishing the same as hunting?

These are complex issues. Many well-meaning people are overwhelmed by the arguments and moral questions and end up doing nothing.

Your activist parents *are* doing something. Does a glimpse into the complexity of animal rights activism help you sympathize with your parents' volunteer work?

If you decide to help, see the back of the book for places where your help is needed.

CHAPTER 14

The Anti-Drug and -Alcohol Activist

I s someone in your home addicted to drugs or alcohol? How do you deal with it? It must be painful and generate fear for your family members.

Perhaps one of your parents has become an activist on the issues of addiction. Can he or she really help, you may often wonder in despair.

Let's look at some of the facts and issues.

Every minute and a half another cocaine addict is born in America. According to a recent congressional report, 375,000 babies who have been exposed to cocaine during pregnancy are born in this country each year. The babies experience no "high"; instead they cry and suffer. Some have heart attacks and die.

Perhaps you already are aware how drugs destroy careers and wreck families (is your activist parent trying to stop this?).

Drug abuse exists not only among a certain group of

people. It is everywhere. One out of three Americans has used illicit drugs, and one in ten uses them regularly.

More than half of all high school seniors use drugs, and more than a quarter use them on a regular basis.

The Media Advertising Partnership for a Drug-Free America reports that one out of six American children ages nine to twelve has been offered drugs.

As for alcoholism, about seventeen million Americans are alcoholics, according to the Will Rogers Institute. Alcoholism does much the same damage as drug abuse: It kills the abusers and innocent people, destroys families, and ruins careers.

Drunk driving alone has become a national problem. The National Highway Traffic Safety Administration states that alcohol-related deaths make up about half of all traffic deaths.

How Can You Cope?

If anyone in your family is an addict and one of your parents is an activist in the desperate hope of helping (if not the person in your family) at least someone, educate yourself.

The more you stay on top of current issues, the more you can be understanding. Knowing the facts will help you to discuss the problems intelligently with friends and family members, and to better express your ideas to your government representatives, should you decide to become involved.

If you are upset that your activist parent has never talked to you about the issues, be adamant in wanting to know. These are not times for family secrets.

If you are the one having a problem with drugs or alcohol, talking about it may not be easy. If you know that your parents know and you can't talk to them, going to a self-help group at least once is not a big sacrifice. Try to understand your parents' love and fears for you.

If you have a friend with an addiction problem, ask your activist parent about places where your friend can get treatment.

Find out in what area of activism your parents are most interested. You are of an age where you can be of help. Cooperating with your mother's or father's work toward a nonaddicted country may bring great excitement as you, too, offer to give something back to society.

CHAPTER 15

Activists for the

Homeless

Help is desperately needed for the homeless. The National Coalition for the Homeless estimates that 3,000,000 Americans may be homeless.

Sadly, the number is increasing. Who are the people with nowhere to live?

After surveying twenty-seven major cities, the U.S. Conference of Mayors found that approximately 25 percent are people with severe mental illness; 4 percent are teenagers who are alone; 14 percent are single women, 24 percent are *employed*, and 26 percent are veterans.

Most of the homeless are under thirty years of age.

You may have thought that people sleeping on the streets and in shelters were middle-aged alcoholic men on Skid Row, but that is not true.

What puts people out of their homes? Often it is a few lost paychecks, a big medical problem, a fire, or some other emergency.

One of the worst aspects is that many homeless families include young children.

Your parents must have educated themselves about the problems of homelessness before becoming activists. Since they have become involved, the phone may be ringing off the hook in your house. Every time you want to call a friend, the phone is already ringing. That would upset most teenagers. What can you decide to do? Could you get a job in a hamburger place, or baby-sit, or offer to cook at home and "buy" a phone for yourself? Then the incessant ringing for your parents wouldn't bother you. What else can you do to cope with such a situation?

If you're interested in learning more, perhaps you could get a copy of *Homelessness in America: A Photographic Project* (Acropolis Books). It is a collection of black-and-white photographs documenting homelessness in our country.

At the core of your being, however, what else could be worrying you? Let's examine some serious questions.

1. Do you think your parents could ever become homeless? Are you worried about what might happen to you?
2. Is the whole idea of your parents' activism scary to you? Are you afraid a mentally ill person may knock on your door when you're alone and you won't know what to do?

There are questions that your parents can answer. They can also point you to reading about our poorest Americans.

Perhaps you can help by not throwing something away. Think about this: Could it be used at a shelter or soup kitchen?

You may find extra bathroom supplies, crutches, food, bedding, eyeglasses, cleaning products, and many other things right in your home.

Shelters with children need toys, games, stuffed animals, and diapers.

Collect a few things for shelters and give them to your parents for distribution. Then tell them of your fears. You'll be well on your way to coping with your activist folks and with your own worries.

You also may feel better knowing that you have contributed.

Calvin Stewart, A Person to Give You Hope

Calvin Stewart was a homeless young man who won a photography scholarship.

He became suddenly homeless in November 1988, after his family had moved to the nation's capital from San Antonio.

Calvin was seventeen years old. He kept a positive attitude and studied hard every day. He didn't know how bad things would get.

Today, however, Calvin is a student at Radford University in Virginia and the recipient of a $1,000 scholarship from a media center, a program for homeless children to express themselves with cameras.

Thanks to an organization called Shooting Back, Calvin became interested in photography. Now he is deciding whether to major in sports medicine or photography or film editing. He plans to go to graduate school. "Hey," he says, "shoot for it, why not?"

Calvin Stewart's photographs were among those exhibited at the Project for Arts.

He said, "You have to be grateful for anything you

have, because you can lose it at any time, and it won't really be your fault."*

- Stewart's attitude helped him cope with his situation. Does his story make you wonder about the activists at Shoot Back who helped him?
- Do you think Calvin Stewart is a special person? Why?
- Whose responsibility are the homeless?

* Myadi Mukenge, "Calvin Stewart." *U.S. News and World Report*, October 8, 1990.

CHAPTER ◇ 16

The Activist Against

Racism

R ight now in our country, there are many people who are not merely prejudiced against those of another race, but perform acts of hate.

There are also many activists trying to help. If your parents are part of that group, what might be some of your coping problems?

If you live in an all-white neighborhood and some of your neighbors are prejudiced, you might be picked on by schoolmates who see people of other races at meetings in your home. Moreover, your parents may have friends of many races. Your white neighbors are fearful and suspicious, and you don't know how to handle your family's "difference."

On the other hand, in an Afro-American neighborhood white activists may attend meetings. If you are black, you may be called "Uncle Tom" and shunned by former friends.

It is not just a black and white issue. Mexicans, South

Americans, Vietnamese, Haitians, Jews all have experienced prejudice and violence.

Now here you are! Your parents, you think, are making life difficult for you. How can you cope with such activism!

In My Next Life

Author Lawrence Thomas writes, "In my next life, I shall certainly aim to come back a white person, a white male."*

He goes on to describe all the evils the white man has committed, from the Crusades in the Middle Ages, to slavery, to the Holocaust during World War II.

Mr. Thomas, who is a professor of philosophy at Syracuse University, has had such experiences as white women quickly locking the car door when he comes down the street.

He tells of the fear of black men. A black man may be dressed in a business suit just as a white man is, but the trust usually goes to the white, he notices.

"Surely," he says, "whites are wrong in thinking that the high crime rate among males justifies their being suspicious of *all* black males."

All this leads to distrust, low self-esteem, and above all, self-hate.

If a man like Mr. Thomas writes such an article and tries through his moral life and activism to raise the consciousness of blacks and whites, what do you think of the people in your neighborhood who make fun of you

*Thomas, Lawrence, "In My Next Life, I'll Be White." *Ebony* Magazine, December 1990.

because your parents, too, are trying to achieve equality among the races?

You may say you have no prejudices or hate. Your parents need not display themselves in the neighborhood.

Are you willing to take a little test? Write down very quickly, without thinking about it for a long time, ten words to complete the blanks below.

1. Afro-Americans are _____, _____, _____, _____, _____, _____, _____, _____, _____, _____.

2. Jews are _____, _____, _____, _____, _____, _____, _____, _____, _____.

3. Chinese are _____, _____, _____, _____, _____, _____, _____, _____, _____.

4. Mexicans are _____, _____, _____, _____, _____, _____, _____, _____, _____.

5. Filipinos are _____, _____, _____, _____, _____, _____, _____, _____, _____.

6. Whites are _____, _____, _____, _____, _____, _____, _____, _____, _____.

What did you find out? What colors did you use to describe them, what jobs did you give them, what character traits did you assign them?

Are you totally free of prejudice, fear, and hate of other races?

The activist does some of the following:

He works toward fair housing, so that minorities are not banned from neighborhoods in which they want to live.

The activist goes to bat for better education for minorities.

The activist works for laws that benefit minorities in the workplace, in jobs, in medical care.

Above all, the activist hopes for the day when Martin Luther King's dream will come true and we will all be simply mankind working and playing together.

What can you do about the jeering of your neighbors? Maybe nothing. But possibly you can take them aside one at a time and tell them of the unfairness and hatred that has promoted so much misery.

Go to your counselor and ask if a program could be given in school regarding racism.

Who knows? One of your parents might be a speaker.

If that happens, you've not only coped with your problem but become a mini-activist yourself.

CHAPTER 17

The Political

Activist

I n fact, most activism is political in nature. Activists work toward having laws changed.

That may not be clear to you, because your parents assume that you know what it's all about and so neglect to tell you exactly what they are doing.

You will be able to think the issues through and cope better with your folks if you are informed.

Your parents may be expressing their views on issues to your government representatives. That is one of the most effective ways to create change. The belief that you cannot make a difference with just one letter, one phone call, is simply false; every opinion is noted. One letter can represent the views of several hundred people, so if your parents are steamed about an issue, they let their representative know about it.

Is your mother a member of the League of Women Voters? That is a nonprofit, nonpartisan organization that encourages the *informed* and *active* participation of citizens in government and influences public policy through education. Your parents are probably involved in Presidential elections, as well as state and city races. If they are political activists, ask them about their candidates, find out what they are looking for in government.

Think about this country, a country where *any* citizen may send a letter to the President, to Senators, and to Congressmen. Your activist parents can complain about laws they find unfair.

Do you complain about family rules that you think unfair? See the similarity?

Your mother and father are just doing it on a larger scale so that fairness prevails.

Let's Look Again at Needs to Cope

As you are becoming better informed about some of the issues in which your parents are activists, you may wonder why you were upset with them in the first place.

Despite the many noble causes, *your* feelings are important in the family. Your needs should not be pushed aside in favor of activism.

However, as you come to realize the importance and magnitude of many of our nation's problems, your discussions with your mother and father may become more sympathetic. You can be understanding while still letting them know what you are unhappy about. Remember that the open, truthful path toward solving family (and other) problems is the best one.

If empathy evolves on both sides, compromises can be reached. That's what coping is all about.

PART ◇ V

SUMMARY

CHAPTER 18

Letting Go of Anger

At the beginning of this book you took a look at the anger you felt at your parents' activism.

Among your feelings was family pressure on you to support or join in your mother's or father's activism.

You examined the hidden costs of activism—how society benefits, but the family may pay.

You had some positive feelings and were proud of your folks. You could understand their concern for the future, as well as for the present.

You also had a look at your negative feelings: jealousy of the time your parents spent away from you. You may have felt guilty about not wanting to participate. At times you were even embarrassed by your parents and were pressured to conform.

Now you have some coping strategies to work with, such as addressing hidden agendas, finding common values, and doing some self-examination.

It is time now, after the family meetings, after talking with friends and counselors, to let go of your anger and replace it with empathy.

Accept your parents.

Create your own code and discover your own values. You'll find out how much "giving" is right for you.

What's right for you feels good, and you have every reason to hold on to good.

Appendix

To Volunteer as an Activist

Community Service
  American Jewish Congress
  1 Lincoln Plaza
  Boston, MA 02111

Food & Friends
  P.O. Box 70601
  Washington, DC 20024

Project Open Hand
  2720 17th Street
  San Francisco, CA 94110

For More Information

American Council for Drug Education
  204 Monroe Street
  Rockville, MD 20850

Bacchus of the U.S., MC
  National Headquarters
  P.O. Box 10430
  Denver, CO 80210

Campuses Without Drugs, Inc.
2530 Holly Drive
Pittsburgh, PA 15235

National Council on Alcoholism and Drug
Dependence Hotline
(7 days a week, 24 hours a day)
1-800-622-2255

The Hope Foundation
1555 Regal Row
Dallas, TX 75247

Homelessness Information Exchange
1830 Connecticut Avenue, NW
Washington, DC 20009

The American Vegan Society
502 Old Harding Highway
Malaga, NJ 08328

The American Society for the
Prevention of Cruelty to Animals
441 East 92nd Street
New York, NY 10128

Sex Information and Education Council of the U.S.
130 West 42nd Street
New York, NY 10030

The Animals Voice Magazine
P.O. Box 16955
North Hollywood, CA 91615-9931

League of Women Voters
  1730 M Street NW
  Washington, DC 20036

The League publishes numerous informative pamphlets, including "Tell It to Washington: Vote!", "The First Steps," "How to Judge a Candidate," "How to Watch a Debate," "Unmet Needs."

For Further Reading

Barry, James H. *Plating the Seeds for the Next 100 Years*. San Francisco, Sierra Club, 1991.

Bettelheim, Bruno. *A Good Enough Parent*. New York: Alfred A. Knopf, 1987.

Cadwallader, Sharon. *The Living Kitchen*. San Francisco: Sierra Club, 1991.

Faber, Adele, and Mazlisch, Elaine. *Liberated Parents and Liberated Children*. New York: Avon Books, 1974.

Ferguson, Marilyn. *The Aquarian Conspiracy*. New York: St. Martins Press 1980.

Fromm, Erich. *Escape from Freedom*. New York: Avon, 1965.

Kunofsky, Judith. *How to Become an Environmental Activist*. San Francisco: Sierra Club,

Paul, Jordan, Ph.D., and Paul, Margaret, Ph.D. *Do I Have to Give Up Me to Be Loved by You?* Minneapolis: CompCare Publications, 1983.

Index

DATE DUE
